ACTORS

ON

ACTORS

IN THE SAME SERIES

WRITERS ON WRITERS

ACTORS

— ON —

ACTORS

COMPILED BY
GRAHAM TARRANT

INTRODUCTION BY
BRYAN FORBES

AURUM PRESS

FOR ABIGAIL SOPHIE, WITH LOVE

FIRST PUBLISHED 1995 BY AURUM PRESS LIMITED

25 BEDFORD AVENUE, LONDON WC1B 3AT

A CATALOGUE RECORD FOR THIS BOOK IS AVAILABLE FROM

THE BRITISH LIBRARY.

ISBN 1 85410 319 9

DESIGNED BY DESIGN/SECTION, FROME

PRINTED BY REGENT PUBLISHING SERVICES LTD

IN HONG KONG

INTRODUCTION

Orson Welles, speaking with the authority born of a self-destructed career, once said, "Every actor in his heart believes everything bad that's printed about him." Few of his fellow actors would refute that harsh verdict. The confidence that the majority of actors are compelled to display in order to get through each day is more often than not a mere facade – yet another mask they don to conceal their basic insecurity. Johnson pronounced us no better than "dancing dogs", Hitchcock thought we should be treated like cattle, long ago we were termed "a despicable race", yet despite these and other, equally scathing, brickbats, all the actors I have ever known have always been prepared to go one step further than their most damning critics and cheerfully exchange premature obituaries.

Humour in the theatre often stems from self-inflicted wounds; we positively delight recounting past failures, knowing beyond doubt that our own turn will come around and that nothing recedes like success. (The actor who enjoys years of household-name status in a long-running television series often finds himself virtually unemployable when the series ends.) Following a personal triumph one actress was heard to remark, "The worst part of success is trying to find somebody who is happy for you," and we all know the truth of that.

But it would be a mistake for outsiders to take such cynical observations at face value; they are merely insurance policies against the day when fortune turns a blind eye, as she is sure to do. Actors feel the need to knock themselves before others do it for them, and this, to my mind, is their ultimate saving grace and excuses many of their conceits.

They are gamblers all, for in the main it is a profession of rejection, a profession of many blessings (the camaraderie of a shared act of creativity, the pleasure of giving pleasure, the rare feeling of being different), yet always a profession where one lives on the edge. Our emotional barometers swing violently between Fair weather and Stormy and, for many, good times will never be around the corner, so the umbrellas are always half-opened in readiness.

In the quotations which follow, the actor reveals his many faces. Often more Caliban than Adonis, he lays bare his hopes, his frustrations, his courage, arrogance and humility in the course of plunging from want into luxury, from basking in the sunlight of transient fortune to the twilight of being passed over. So as you read this engaging collection call to mind the words of Richard Garnett, who asked us to "have patience with the jealousies and petulance of actors, for their hour is their eternity."

Bryan Forbes

When Kean came on I was astonished. I was prepared to see a small man; but, diminished by the unusual distance and his black dress, and a mental comparison with Kemble's princely person, he appeared a perfect pigmy; his voice unlike any I had ever heard before, perhaps from its very strangeness, was most objectionable… I quietly gazed on through three tedious scenes – for all the actors seemed worse than usual – till it came to the dialogue with the ghost, and at the line "I'll call thee Hamlet – king – father", I was converted.

JOSEPH COWEN ON EDMUND KEAN, 1814

Kean possesses particular physical qualifications – an eye like an orb of light, a voice exquisitely melodious in its tenderness, and in the harsh dissonance of vehement passion terribly true. To these he adds the intellectual one of vigour, intensity, amazing powers of concentrating effect: these give him an entire mastery over his audience in all striking, sudden, impassioned passages, in fulfilling which he has contented himself; leaving unheeded what he probably could not compass – the unity of conception, refinement of detail and evenness of execution.

FANNY KEMBLE ON EDMUND KEAN, 1832

Ellen Terry was very much a daughter of Shakespeare and when she spoke his prose it was as though she was only repeating something she had heard him say to her in the next room, and would then come straight onto the stage and say it.

GORDON CRAIG ON ELLEN TERRY

Gertrude Lawrence at her best, and with me she was usually at her best, was the most brilliant comedienne to play with. She was so swift and her eyes were so true; it was an enchantment to work with her. Her use of voice was instinctive. Gertie was not a thinking reed, but her talent gave it all to her. She was intuitive and accurate, when she did not occasionally go overboard, which she was inclined to do.

NOËL COWARD ON GERTRUDE LAWRENCE

As a craftsman, as a technician, there was nothing he could not do. His comedy timing was absolutely spot on.

ERIC PORTER ON DONALD WOLFIT

He was one of those actors who just seemed to draw the best out of you because in a scene his concentration was entirely on you, and he was the character he was playing.

VIRGINIA MCKENNA ON PETER FINCH

Spencer Tracy was the first actor I've ever seen who could just look down in the dirt and command a scene. He played a set-up with Robert Ryan [in *Bad Day at Black Rock*] that way. He's looking down at the road and then he looks at Ryan at just the precise, right minute. I tell you, Rob could've stood on his head and zipped open his fly and the scene would still have been Mr Tracy's.

ERNEST BORGNINE

Spence is the best we have, because you don't see the mechanism at work.

HUMPHREY BOGART ON SPENCER TRACY

I learned about acting just sitting there night after night, watching Henry Fonda. That man's a total actor.

JAMES GARNER
(who had a non-speaking part in the stage version of
The Caine Mutiny, *starring Fonda)*

He once told me that a great actor has to be a magpie: he must steal everything. So Larry stole the clipped delivery from Ronald Colman – he even stole Ronald Colman's thin moustache. You listen to Ronald Colman saying *Shangri-La* and compare it with that febrile tenor of Larry's in *And. now. is. the win. ter. of. our. dis. con. tent…* It is the same.

ROBERT STEPHENS ON LAURENCE OLIVIER

He brought a tremendous understanding to parts and could convey hidden complexities, not just playing the moment, but conveying many layers of thought at the same time. He was definitely among the top ten actors of his age group.

ALAN BATES ON IAN CHARLESON

Even when he made a visible effort to play a love scene, he always gave the impression he was wearing only one shoe and looking for the other while he slowly droned his lines.

MARLENE DIETRICH ON JAMES STEWART

Sir Alec's masterly character creations can be likened to the artistry of that great painter Seurat, who built each detail of colour and shape on his canvas by a series of tiny dots, which blend with thousands of other tiny dots to achieve the complete interpretation. Such painstaking artistic creativity lies at the heart of his genius.

IAN RICHARDSON ON ALEC GUINNESS

The thing he does brilliantly, and he's the only person able to do it – except for Anthony Hopkins, who does it now – is to apparently do absolutely nothing in a close-up, and you know what he is thinking.

EILEEN ATKINS ON ALEC GUINNESS

Clint Eastwood appears to do nothing and does everything, reducing everything and everybody – like Mitchum and Tracy.

RICHARD BURTON

When you work with other actors, something happens in the eyes as they start to assume the characters. The eyes grow grey and glassy, the way a snake looks just before it is going to shed its skin. Actors *start acting*. But Marlon never did. He *was* Terry Malloy [in *On the Waterfront*].

EVA MARIE SAINT ON MARLON BRANDO

When you look in his eyes when you're acting opposite him, it's a hell of a thing. It's like hands that come out and grab you by your face. He's powerful, *very* strong. He takes it up another level, so *you* gotta take it up too. If you don't, people won't even notice that you're on screen.

CHAZZ PALMINTERI ON ROBERT DE NIRO

He is a wizard… He can blush or turn white just like that!

SHELLEY WINTERS ON ROBERT DE NIRO

Take one, Bobby's getting orientated. By ten, you're watching magic, and in fifteen, you're seeing genius.

JERRY LEWIS ON ROBERT DE NIRO

A lot of actors would say, "Give me time to find myself emotionally." But a guy like Hoskins will just sit there in the back of a car with the director taking him through those moments as they occur, as the director conjures them, and play them with such effortlessness and concentration that you buy it. All those feelings compressed into a few minutes of film. It was remarkable.

A. MARTINEZ ON BOB HOSKINS

If I know anything about movie acting, it's from practising my Burt Lancaster sneer – from *Vera Cruz* – at 16 in front of a bedroom mirror.

SAM SHEPARD

Behind the Mask

The mild and modest expression of his Italian features, and his unassuming manner, which I might perhaps justly describe as partaking in some degree of shyness, took one by surprise… He was very sparing of words during, and for some time after, supper; but about one o'clock, when the glass had circulated pretty freely, he became animated, fluent, and communicative. His anecdotes were related with a lively sense of the ridiculous; in the melodies he sang there was a touching grace, and his powers of mimicry were most humorously or happily exerted.

WILLIAM CHARLES MACREADY ON EDMUND KEAN, 1815

I called on him at Cheltenham. It had been said that he was not over-polite to some of the profession, and in a general way that he was exclusive and difficult of approach. I found him the opposite of all this; a fine, distinguished old man, white hair, very courteous, and with a most pleasant smile, a trifle melancholy perhaps… He said he did not believe in an actor remaining on the stage after his powers were at an end; he thought a man should retire in the zenith of his strength;

and he believed he had played Macbeth on that last night as well as ever he had played it.

J.L. TOOLE ON WILLIAM CHARLES MACREADY

She could be wise and even affectionate, and why she had to be so ill-behaved, sometimes even common and rude, it was difficult to tell. A kind of demon seized her and she could not resist being unkind to people, making cheap jokes at their expense. Yet she could also be witty, very lady-like and gracious.

JOHN GIELGUD ON MRS PATRICK CAMPBELL

He was a rare human being. Very intellectual, very intelligent. I don't think that came across in his screen personality. He was an awful tease. He could really upset people, turn them upside down and make them cry. But it was usually deserved. He came out and said what he felt. He knew phonies, and he hated phonies.

CLAIRE TREVOR ON HUMPHREY BOGART

She has the enormous eyes which can be very frightening but if you look into them there's something also very haunted and frightened in them; in playing a scene she reached a point and then you saw her eyes do something and she seemed to go off into something surreal. It happened in her films and that made her feel that it might have happened in her life; that she went into a place that she didn't know where she was.

FAYE DUNAWAY ON JOAN CRAWFORD

She had such intelligence, beauty and style. She never left the stage-door unless impeccably dressed... She was always amusing. And she was honest, totally and utterly honest... She was a woman, and yet always somehow a child.

PETER WYNGARDE ON VIVIEN LEIGH

When she was good, she was very, very good, but when she was bad, she was *awful*.

MAXINE AUDLEY ON VIVIEN LEIGH

He was ambitious, full of guile and had the air of an arrogant dandy. But a small uncertain boy hid behind the mask... His insecurity showed in some infuriating ways. He was incapable of sitting down in a restaurant without sending the food back, sometimes before it reached the table, and he always carried his own cold Chablis with him, as he drank nothing else.

JOSS ACKLAND ON LAURENCE HARVEY

She simply isn't like other people. If we were all in the same building and it began to fall down, we'd all run. But Marilyn would probably run in a totally different direction. But the point is, she wouldn't get hit by any falling bricks because she's not only different, she's smart.

JACK LEMMON ON MARILYN MONROE

Chaplin was probably the most sadistic man I'd ever met. He was an egotistical tyrant and a penny-pincher who never wanted to spend a nickel, constantly harassed people when they were late, and scolded them unmercifully to work faster.

MARLON BRANDO ON CHARLIE CHAPLIN

He had a wonderful sense of humour, but I was very frightened of him. He could be distressingly autocratic and dismissive.

MICHAEL HORDERN ON RALPH RICHARDSON

Witty, sophisticated and infinitely debonair, in life a prey to theosophical charlatans, socially insecure, and inclined to isolation.

GEORGE SANDERS ON CARY GRANT

The most charming, persuasive bastard ever to draw breath.

PETER O'TOOLE ON LAURENCE OLIVIER

I've always thought we were the reverse of the same coin…the top half John – all spiritual, all spirituality, all beauty, all abstract things; and myself all earth, blood, everything to do with earth, humanity if you like – the baser part of humanity.

LAURENCE OLIVIER ON JOHN GIELGUD

He can do anything. A bit cuckoo, but sweet and terribly funny.

KATHARINE HEPBURN ON PETER O'TOOLE

I'm here to speak about his wit, his charm, his warmth, his talent… At last a real acting job!

BURT LANCASTER ON KIRK DOUGLAS

Boastful, egotistical, resentful of criticism – if anyone dare give it.

JOAN FONTAINE ON KIRK DOUGLAS

You won't find anything wrong with him. But if you do, for heaven's sake let the rest of us know.

SIDNEY POITIER ON JACK LEMMON

Bob is a private man, so it takes a long time to get to know him. He is a man obsessed with his work and who continually worries.

JEREMY IRONS ON ROBERT DE NIRO

When she's good, she's divinely good; but when she's bad — oh, my God!

HERBERT BEERBOHM TREE ON MRS PATRICK CAMPBELL

God was very good to the world. He took her from us.

BETTE DAVIS ON MIRIAM HOPKINS

Douglas has always faced a situation in the only way he knew how, by running away from it.

MARY PICKFORD ON DOUGLAS FAIRBANKS

Say anything you like, but don't say I love to work. That sounds like Mary Pickford, that prissy bitch!

MABEL NORMAND

Miss Bankhead isn't well enough known nationally to warrant my imitating her.

BETTE DAVIS ON TALLULAH BANKHEAD

Surely no one but a mother could have loved Bette Davis at the height of her career.

BRIAN AHERNE ON BETTE DAVIS

If this child had been born in the Middle Ages, she'd have been burned as a witch.

LIONEL BARRYMORE ON MARGARET O'BRIEN

Olivier is a *tour de force*, Wolfit is forced to tour.

HERMIONE GINGOLD

We all thought he was a joke.

JOHN GIELGUD ON DONALD WOLFIT

My doctor won't let me watch Dinah [Shore]. I'm a diabetic.

OSCAR LEVANT

Poor old rotten egg Joan. I kept my mouth shut about her for nearly a quarter of a century, but she was a mean, tipsy, powerful, rotten-egg lady.

MERCEDES McCAMBRIDGE ON JOAN CRAWFORD

I can't honestly say that Esther Williams ever acted in an Andy Hardy picture, but she swam in one.

MICKEY ROONEY

Dietrich? That *contraption*! She was one of the beautiful-but-dumb girls, like me, but she belonged to the category of those who thought they were smart and fooled other people into believing it.

LOUISE BROOKS ON MARLENE DIETRICH

She looked as if butter wouldn't melt in her mouth – or anywhere else.

ELSA LANCHESTER ON MAUREEN O'HARA

I knew Doris Day before she was a virgin.

OSCAR LEVANT

If you were more of a woman, I would be more of a man. Kissing you is like kissing the side of a beer bottle.

LAURENCE HARVEY ON CAPUCINE

Acting with Harvey is like acting by yourself – but worse.

JANE FONDA ON LAURENCE HARVEY

As wistful as an iron foundry.

OSCAR LEVANT ON DEBBIE REYNOLDS

She's common, she can't act – yet she's the hottest female property around these days. If that doesn't tell you something about the state of our industry today, what does?

STEWART GRANGER ON JOAN COLLINS

I'm No 10 [at the box office]. Right under Barbra Streisand. Can you imagine being *under* Barbra Streisand? Get me a bag, I may throw up.

WALTER MATTHAU

She's a ball-buster. Protect me from her.

NICK NOLTE ON BARBRA STREISAND

Meryl Streep is an acting machine in the same sense that a shark is a killing machine.

CHER

I think in the future she should be playing horny old aunts.

OLIVER REED ON GLENDA JACKSON

Conduct Un̬becoming

When he had played a part for a few weeks he would begin to tire and get mischievous and slack. He would forget his words; his mind would be crowded with thoughts of the new production. Then there would be frantic people in the wings with his cues chalked on a blackboard in huge letters for him to see, or somebody under the table prompting him, or in the fireplace, or bits of his part, written on paper, would be pinned behind the furniture.

CONSTANCE COLLIER ON HERBERT BEERBOHM TREE

It takes an earthquake to get Jack out of bed, a flood to make him wash, and the United States Army to put him to work.

LIONEL BARRYMORE ON JOHN BARRYMORE

Carole Lombard was a wonderful girl. Swore like a man. Other women try, but she really did.

FRED MACMURRAY

I don't have a fond memory of Mae West. She did her own thing to the detriment of everyone around her.

CARY GRANT

Her manner to me got steadily ruder and more insolent; whenever I patiently laboured to make her understand an indication for some reading, business or timing she would listen with ill-disguised impatience, and when I had finished would turn to Paula [Strasberg, her drama coach] and petulantly demand, "Wasseee mean?" A very short way into the filming, my humiliation had reached depths I would not have believed possible.

LAURENCE OLIVIER ON MARILYN MONROE
(filming The Prince and the Showgirl*)*

When he was sober he was a delight to work with. He learned his dance steps like lightning but on his bad days I can't remember anyone so terrible. He arrived for work no earlier than noon, unchanged and unshaved, just in time for the picnic lunch that had been provided for the cast.

ANNA NEAGLE ON ERROL FLYNN

He went fishing and fucking, and paid no attention to his talent.

VIVECA LINDFORS ON ERROL FLYNN

[Filming *55 Days at Peking*] Today marked the worst behaviour I've yet seen from that curious breed I make my living opposite. Ava showed up for a late call, did one shot (with the usual incredible delay in coming to the set), and then walked off just before lunch when some Chinese extra took a still of her. She came back after a painful three-hour lunch break…only to walk off again, for the same reason (this time untrue; the Chinese extra did *not* take a still of her).

CHARLTON HESTON ON AVA GARDNER,
Journal, 1 September 1962

Doris Day is one of the most difficult actresses I've met. She spent so much time crying.

DAVID NIVEN

He is constantly demanding that scenes be rewritten. You never knew where the hell you were; you wouldn't know for ten minutes what you were playing because the next scene contradicted it.

TREVOR HOWARD ON MARLON BRANDO

He is difficult and boring. He doesn't play a scene with you – everything's secret. He doesn't pour on the coal in the first take, but lets it go on to the eleventh and suddenly it clicks for him. "That's it", he says and walks off. Meanwhile your best take may have been number three. It's a self-centred sort of art.

RICHARD HARRIS ON MARLON BRANDO

It shows that it doesn't take intelligence to be a good actor.

GREGORY PECK ON MARLON BRANDO

(after the latter had arranged for an "Apache militant" to take his place at the Oscars ceremony and decline his award for The Godfather*)*

For one so richly talented, she appeared curiously over-wary of young performers. Louise Purnell and I were playing Sorrel and Simon [in *Hay Fever*]; she was jealous of our getting laughs. She'd send us little notes to come and see her and then tell us not to do things. She made us feel constrained.

DEREK JACOBI ON EDITH EVANS

Roger [Moore] behaves like a schoolboy let loose in a fun palace: he will swing from ropes, slide down bannisters, squirt water, let off smoke-bombs, set wind-machines in motion… Once the clapper-board clicks, however, he becomes painstaking and professional, but with all his professionalism, he clearly regards the whole exercise as fun.

TOPOL

I have never met anyone so badly behaved.

JAMES MASON ON RAQUEL WELCH

L👁 👁ks are Everything

His eyes are marvellous, having a sort of fascination, like that attributed to the snake.

SARAH SIDDONS ON EDMUND KEAN

I have never in any face, in any country, seen such wonderful eyes.

ELLEN TERRY ON EDWIN BOOTH

He is both manly and wistful. He wins the sympathy of women because his face expresses tenderness and silent suffering.

NORMA SHEARER ON HERBERT MARSHALL

Claude Rains was one of the best actors I worked with. As a leading man he was difficult to cast… He was very short and would be made to stand on a pile of books.

FLORA ROBSON

She had wonderful *eyes* – expressive. On the stage she had an extraordinary concentration and she had a wealth of emotion to *concentrate*.

RALPH RICHARDSON ON FLORA ROBSON

His great basic quality was a splendid roughness. Even when perfectly groomed I felt I could have lit a match on his jaw.

PETER USTINOV ON HUMPHREY BOGART

I have just come from the Actor's Studio where I saw Marilyn Monroe. She had no girdle on, her ass was hanging out. She is a disgrace to the industry.

JOAN CRAWFORD

There's a broad with a future behind her.

CONSTANCE BENNETT ON MARILYN MONROE

Looks like she could be a cold dish with a man until you get her pants down and then she'd explode.

GARY COOPER ON GRACE KELLY

I'm getting older too. The only one who isn't is Cary Grant.

GRACE KELLY

Have you ever noticed his eyes? They look right through you! I met him once and he looked into my eyes, right down inside me, looked around, and there was no one there, so he walked away.

FRED GWYNNE ON RICHARD BURTON

You know you can't act, and if you hadn't been so good-looking you would never have gotten a picture.

KATHARINE HEPBURN ON ROBERT MITCHUM

Joanne Woodward is setting the cause of Hollywood glamour back twenty years by making her own clothes.

JOAN CRAWFORD

People who wanted to be nice about my looks always would say: "You remind me so much of Bette Davis." Very nice, except I can't stand Bette Davis.

JEANNE MOREAU

I think he's got a pair of the best eyes that have ever been seen on screen, apart from anything else he might have that's good and there's plenty of that!

HONOR BLACKMAN ON SEAN CONNERY

He is very nice to snog. That mouth! Just like a black man's.

ANNA CHANCELLOR ON MARTIN CLUNES

MIXED NOTICES

Coghlan's Shylock was not even bad. It was nothing. You could hardly hear a word he said. He spoke as though he had a sponge in his mouth, and moved as if paralysed. The perspiration poured down his face; yet what he was doing no one could guess. It was a case of moral cowardice rather than incompetency. At rehearsals no one had entirely believed in him, and this, instead of stinging him into a resolution to triumph, had made him take fright and run away. People felt they were witnessing a great play with a great part cut out.

ELLEN TERRY ON CHARLES COGHLAN

Henry Irving's Othello was condemned almost as universally as his Iago was praised… He screamed and ranted and raved – lost his voice, was slow where he should have been swift, incoherent where he should have been strong. I could not bear to see him in the part. It was painful to me. Yet night after night he achieved in the speech to the Senate one of the most superb and beautiful bits of acting of his life.

ELLEN TERRY

I remember so vividly his coming across the stage for his final entrance [as Becket]. I remember that he trailed one foot a little and this most significant and most moving appearance greatly affected me. When he came to his death scene I actually fainted in my seat.

ATHENE SEYLER ON HENRY IRVING

The loveliest performance I ever saw was Ellen Terry as Imogen. When she entered I felt she had come from the moon: when she left the stage I was sure the stars were greeting her. No one has ever had her magical step – that extraordinary happy haste that made you feel she must presently arrive at the gates of Paradise.

MRS PATRICK CAMPBELL

With his Lear, when he cursed Goneril, one trembled. I trembled in the theatre. I was petrified of what was going to happen, because he certainly had influence with the gods. I thought: there will be a flash of lightning and Goneril will disappear. Astonishing. I'd never believed an actor could be that big. It was like listening to Beethoven's Ninth or looking at Michelangelo's *Last Judgement* in the Sistine Chapel.

DONALD SINDEN ON DONALD WOLFIT

I thought, surely she won't come over, she's so small scale, but when I saw her on the screen [in *The Prince and the Showgirl*], my goodness how it came over. She was a revelation. We theatre people tend to be so outgoing. She was the reverse. The perfect film actress.

DAME SYBIL THORNDIKE ON MARILYN MONROE

In 1957 I saw Peggy Ashcroft in *Cymbeline*. The beauty and grace of her Imogen was so overpowering that I fancied it was all for my benefit alone. I had seen Dame Peggy up close when I got her autograph and knew that she was, in life, old enough to be Imogen's mother. But from the back of the stalls, she was essential youth in voice and gesture.

IAN MCKELLEN

Alec [Guinness, in Terence Rattigan's play *Ross*] looked very like Lawrence of Arabia and played it well enough, but there was something lacking. He has a certain dullness about him and his "big" moment seemed contrived. He also wore a blonde "piece" which was too bright and remained blandly intact even after he had been beaten up and buggered by twelve Turks.

NOËL COWARD,
Diary, 15 May 1960

I think Alec and I made a good team [in *The Lavender Hill Mob*] because when he is playing comedy I think he is at his best when he has another comic personality to play against, to set off his own performance. On his own – and I stress I mean in comedy, not necessarily serious roles – he needs to disguise to help him.

STANLEY HOLLOWAY ON ALEC GUINNESS

I saw Shelley Winters in *A Place in the Sun*. She gave a very moving performance, which surprised me, because Shelley is not a sensitive girl socially.

JOAN CRAWFORD

We had one week [filming *I Could Go On Singing*], one final week which she did for me, of complete, unforgettable magic. She was on time every day, her work was brilliant, we tore into the scenes and she blasted off the screen. My final day was our big scene. We started together rehearsing in her dressing room at eight-thirty... We rehearsed for six hours, with half an hour for a sandwich, in the cramped little caravan. At four-thirty we went on to the floor and shot the entire scene just once. It lasted eight minutes and was one of the most perfect moments of supreme screen acting I have ever witnessed. I shall never see its like again. She never put a foot wrong, not an effect was missed, the overlaps, the stumbling, the range, above all the brilliance of her range...from black farce right through to black tragedy, a cadenza of pain and suffering, of bald, unvarnished truth.

DIRK BOGARDE ON JUDY GARLAND

A Steve McQueen performance just naturally lends itself to monotony. Steve doesn't bring much to the party.

ROBERT MITCHUM

Peter [O'Toole] doesn't seem to realise that we do Shakespeare far more quickly now, without laboriously explaining the setting of each scene… Doing the play this way, he's not being fair to himself. He's got a wonderful Macbeth in him. We all know that. It's sad that he rejects any direction advice.

TIMOTHY WEST

(on O'Toole's heavily panned Macbeth, 1980)

I never went for the Welsh-wizardry and didn't like the way he cultivated or acquired the Olivier mannerisms – the sudden fortissimos, the instant access to the emotions, and all the characteristics of the shouting school of acting.

ALAN BENNETT ON RICHARD BURTON

On the night I went to see Ian's Hamlet at the National there were a lot of sixth-formers in the theatre, who can be a tricky audience, but from the first soliloquy Ian captured them. At the end nearly everyone rose to their feet and cheered, something I've never seen at any performance of Shakespeare. That was an audience unifying. It's a very powerful thing. And Ian did that through his art, through his soul. Even if people didn't really know what was being touched on, something very deep and primal had happened.

SUZANNE BERTISH ON IAN CHARLESON

Something
EXTRA

She stood alone on her height of excellence. Her acting was perfection, and as I recall it I do not wonder, novice as I was, at my perturbation when on the stage with her.

WILLIAM CHARLES MACREADY ON SARAH SIDDONS
(acting with her for the first time, 1811)

This great and overwhelming artist was almost too individual, too exotic, to be completely understood or properly estimated *all at once*. Her superb diction, her lovely silken voice, her natural acting, her passionate temperament, her fire – in a word, transcendent genius – caused amazement. She filled the imagination as a great poet might do.

LILLIE LANGTRY ON SARAH BERNHARDT

No-one plays a love-scene better, but it is a picture of love that she gives, a strange orchidaceous picture rather than a suggestion of the ordinary human passion as felt by ordinary people. She is exotic. Well, what else could she be?

ELLEN TERRY ON SARAH BERNHARDT

People tried to delude the world into believing that he was a great artist, a great personality, a great anything you like, but they would never admit the great actor.

GORDON CRAIG ON HENRY IRVING

He gave so much of himself to every performance that each one seemed a chip off his life. He was really obsessed when on the stage, where not a bit of the off-stage Jack existed! Acting had the most extraordinary physical effect on him.

CONSTANCE COLLIER ON JOHN BARRYMORE

[John] Barrymore was one of the very few who had that divine madness without which a great artist cannot work or live.

GRETA GARBO

Professionally he's easy to rate. He was the best. There were no long-winded arguments in Broadway cafés. Walter Huston just happened to be the best, that's all.

SPENCER TRACY

He was one of the few men I've ever known who was proud of being an actor. He thought acting was a fine profession. His work was based a little on his personality. I don't mean in a cute or affected way. It was an actor functioning.

KATHARINE HEPBURN ON HUMPHREY BOGART

People used to comment on what they called his idiosyncrasies, his little foibles. But Coop never made a movie that wasn't thoroughly thought out and planned. He is probably the finest motion picture actor I ever worked with.

ROBERT PRESTON ON GARY COOPER

The only actor of genius I've ever met.

LAURENCE OLIVIER ON CHARLES LAUGHTON

There are very few great actors at any time. Spencer was one of them… There was a light inside that man. It did a positive disservice to some of the movies he was put into. He made them look even shoddier than they were.

KATHARINE HEPBURN ON SPENCER TRACY

There's nobody in the business who can touch him and you're a fool to try. And the bastard knows it, so don't fall for that humble stuff.

CLARK GABLE ON SPENCER TRACY

Everything she does on the stage is interpreted through her own morality. It's the way Picasso paints. It's the way Beethoven composed. It's the thing the great artist has that makes him different from other people.

MICHAEL REDGRAVE ON EDITH EVANS

I remember Olivier as a young actor. He was very noisy. He had no trace of subtlety. He shouted every part. Yet I knew instinctively he'd be a great actor.

CEDRIC HARDWICKE ON LAURENCE OLIVIER

After I've seen Sir Laurence Olivier play a great Shakespearian part, I think I have heard the tongues of angels. There is acting, and there is great acting – and there is the wide world between.

CELIA JOHNSON

Gielgud is the greatest intellectual actor of my time. Olivier was mercurial. [Ralph] Richardson had magic, real magic. Wolfit had grandeur.

DONALD SINDEN

When I have seen him and talked with him, I feel like a plant that has been watered.

MARLENE DIETRICH ON ORSON WELLES

All the tough talk is a blind. He's a very fine man with wonderful manners and he speaks beautifully – when he wants to… Bob would make the best Macbeth of any actor living.

CHARLES LAUGHTON ON ROBERT MITCHUM

Elizabeth would be so good as Lady Macbeth.

RICHARD BURTON ON ELIZABETH TAYLOR

I'm a good actor; Albert Finney is talented; so's Peter O'Toole – all of us of that generation. But there is a special word for people like Brando, and it's genius.

ROBERT STEPHENS ON MARLON BRANDO

There's something about Brando on the screen that galvanises your attention in a way that the other people that come near him, play scenes with him, seem to be just secondary figures in the landscape.

KEVIN MCCARTHY ON MARLON BRANDO

I would like to work with Brando, just to say thanks.

ANTHONY HOPKINS

He is that unique creature who could be an international superstar, perhaps *the* international superstar and billionaire, if he chose to follow the tempting fingers that constantly beckoned to him from every direction. It is almost disturbing to encounter this degree of creative loyalty, this joyful and satisfying integrity.

JOSEPH COTTEN ON PAUL SCOFIELD

I had first seen O'Toole some years ago playing Edmund in *Lear* at the Bristol Old Vic... He looked like a beautiful, emaciated secretary bird. He was extremely young and his acting was unformed and half-derivative, but his voice had a crack like a whip. And, most important of all, you couldn't take your eyes off him.

RICHARD BURTON ON PETER O'TOOLE

Meryl Streep is the greatest living actor that America has, man or woman.

BRUCE WILLIS

In his mouth the worst banalities become poetry. On stage, he flowers. Wherever he is, that is where the action begins.

JEAN CARMET ON GÉRARD DEPARDIEU

I think Hopkins is the best English-speaking actor today. The mantle of Olivier will rest on him if he doesn't get too commercial.

GEORGE C.SCOTT ON ANTHONY HOPKINS

Quality

[**C**harles Laughton] regarded acting as part art and part whoring. He had sold his soul to Hollywood, in a way, but had kept a grip on his impenetrable integrity through thick and thin, playing roles as improbable as American admirals in 'B' pictures, but, when the occasion demanded it, able to hold an audience spellbound by readings from the Bible with no props apart from the hypnotic calm of his personality, his eye flicking like the ignition light on a car, an indication that the engine was still running and would spring into action at any moment.

PETER USTINOV

My idea of a movie star is Joan Crawford, who can chew up two directors and three producers before lunch.

SHELLEY WINTERS

Brynner arrived in Madrid to take over the part of Solomon. Inspired no doubt by the grandeur of the role, he also brought an entourage of seven. The function of one member of this retinue appeared to consist entirely of placing already lighted cigarettes in Brynner's outstretched fingers. Another was permanently occupied in shaving his skull with an electric razor whenever the suspicion of a shadow darkened that noble head.

GEORGE SANDERS ON YUL BRYNNER

Wayne was not a bright or exciting type. He confessed to me that he never read books. But that didn't prevent him from accumulating a nice pile of money over the years. It proves that you don't have to be terribly brilliant to become a great film star.

MARLENE DIETRICH ON JOHN WAYNE

She was the first woman who challenged the old Hollywood system of packaging and gift wrapping the goods in the way *they* wanted and not the way *you* might like it.

FAYE DUNAWAY ON BETTE DAVIS

Bette Davis says: "My name goes above the title. I am a star." Yes, she is a star, and a great one. But is it worth playing all those demented old ladies to maintain that status?

MYRNA LOY

Whatever Bette had chosen to do in life she would have had to be the top or she couldn't have endured it.

GARY MERRILL ON BETTE DAVIS

One of the easiest and most uncomplicated actors I've ever worked with. He had a true sense of life and always saw the humour of our profession.

RITA TUSHINGHAM ON PETER FINCH

Not only a great actor but also a man who made hearts beat faster – the perfect seducer, the man for whom the word "charisma" could have been invented.

MARLENE DIETRICH ON RICHARD BURTON

They called her the "perfect wife" in the movies. I thought she was the perfect movie star.

HENRY FONDA ON MYRNA LOY

I was astonished to find that she's a real pro. She's not afraid to take chances in front of people. Usually, stars become very protective of themselves and very self-indulgent, but she's got a lot of guts. She'd go ahead and explore and risk falling on her face.

PAUL NEWMAN ON ELIZABETH TAYLOR

We had dinner with him. We're driving home and I'm thinking: God, here's old Paul – what is he, 60, 61? He looks great, feels great, has a lot of money, gives to great causes, he's in love with his wife, he races his cars when he wants to, makes a movie when he wants to, he's incredibly happy and still has the face that looks the way it did when he was 20. God, by the time we got home, I wanted to shoot myself.

ROBERT REDFORD ON PAUL NEWMAN

Bob Redford is a star in the shower. No water spray would dare hassle him. The water would never be too hot or too cold and the eggs at breakfast would always come out of the pan perfect.

PAUL NEWMAN ON ROBERT REDFORD

When you are with Sean you learn pretty quickly your place in the galaxy.

KEVIN COSTNER ON SEAN CONNERY

Strictly Personal

Oh how can I act with a dreadful ugly face like that?

MRS PATRICK CAMPBELL ON GERALD DU MAURIER

Norma [Shearer], now a pretty young widow, wasn't getting the love she needed. And she didn't give up. She made it very clear to me, once we were back in Hollywood, that she wanted me. She was hotter than a half-fucked fox in a forest fire.

MICKEY ROONEY

I never knew a man who smelled as wonderfully as he did. I don't know if it was the cologne or his soap or maybe it was a combination of both and especially his own outdoorsy smell. I almost swooned like a heroine in a Victorian novel.

SHELLEY WINTERS ON ERROL FLYNN

What do you know about men, you fat, ugly faggot.

HENRY FONDA ON CHARLES LAUGHTON

He's so full of shit and fury signifying nothing.

CHARLES LAUGHTON ON HENRY FONDA

I hated that bastard.

WILLIAM HOLDEN ON HUMPHREY BOGART

My God, you know I love Pa, but I can't say he's a helluva lay.

CAROLE LOMBARD ON CLARK GABLE

The worst lay in the world – she was always drunk and never stopped eating.

PETER LAWFORD ON RITA HAYWORTH

I don't mean to speak ill of the dead, but he was a prick.

ROCK HUDSON ON JAMES DEAN

We never became lovers, but we could have – like that.

SAL MINEO ON JAMES DEAN

Like Blanche [in *A Streetcar Named Desire*], she slept with almost everybody… I might have given her a tumble if it hadn't been for Larry Olivier. I'm sure he knew she was playing around but, like a lot of husbands I've known, he pretended not to see it, and I liked him too much to invade his chicken coop.

MARLON BRANDO ON VIVIEN LEIGH

Excuse me, Ma'am, I thought you were a guy I knew in Philadelphia.

GROUCHO MARX ON GRETA GARBO

One thing about Steve, he didn't like the women in his life to have balls.

ALI MCGRAW ON STEVE MCQUEEN

I dig my father. I wish he could open his eyes and dig me.

PETER FONDA ON HENRY FONDA

They are trying to show he's a great lover, but they'll never prove it to me.

ZSA ZSA GABOR ON CARY GRANT

If you weren't the best light comedian in the country, all you'd be fit for would be the selling of cars in Great Portland Street.

NOËL COWARD ON REX HARRISON

He's the *most* terrifying perfectionist about what he wants. As an artist I love him. As a husband I *hate* him.

GENA ROWLANDS ON JOHN CASSAVETES

But you can't have him, he's got such a peculiar voice.

EDITH EVANS ON KENNETH WILLIAMS

She is not even an actress…only a trollop.

GLORIA SWANSON ON LANA TURNER

She's just a cranky old broad who's a lot of fun.

NICK NOLTE ON KATHARINE HEPBURN

I always thought that Frank would end up sleeping with a boy.

AVA GARDNER ON FRANK SINATRA
(and his marriage to Mia Farrow)

I have a steak at home, why should I go out for a hamburger?

PAUL NEWMAN ON JOANNE WOODWARD

You're doing it the wrong way round, my boy. You're a star and you don't know how to act.

CEDRIC HARDWICKE ON RICHARD CHAMBERLAIN

Derek, you will always be a fine actor but you'll never be a great actor until you are circumcised.

NOËL COWARD ON DEREK JACOBI

He doesn't need women. They need him, and he's very graceful with that fact.

HELEN MIRREN ON LIAM NEESON

She is a gutsy little bird, a gorgeous snot-nose. I adore her.

PETER O'TOOLE ON JODIE FOSTER

I'm always trying to find diplomatic ways to talk about Richard and the movie *An Officer and a Gentleman*. I liked him before we started but that is the last time I can remember talking to him.

DEBRA WINGER ON RICHARD GERE

W♥rking T♥gether

He growls and prowls, and roams and foams, about the stage, in every direction, like a tiger in his cage, so that I never know on what side of me he means to be; and keeps up a perpetual snarling and grumbling, so that I never feel quite sure that he has done, and that it is my turn to speak... I quail at the idea of his laying hold of me in those terrible passionate scenes; for in *Macbeth* he pinched me black and blue, and almost tore the point lace from my head. I am sure my little finger will be re-broken.

FANNY KEMBLE ON WILLIAM CHARLES MACREADY

When a play was a failure – and that was very rare – he was cheerful and full of good humour. He hated long runs and was always dying to do something new. If a play was succeeding too well and making too much money so that he could not take it off, he was the gloomiest person imaginable because he could not start fresh rehearsals and get to work on new ideas.

CONSTANCE COLLIER ON HERBERT BEERBOHM TREE

I gave up being serious about making pictures about the time I made a film with Greer Garson and she took 125 takes to say no.

ROBERT MITCHUM

Marilyn was an incredible person to act with…the most marvellous I ever worked with, and I have been working for 29 years.

MONTGOMERY CLIFT ON MARILYN MONROE

The title [*The Misfits*] sums up this mess. Miller, Monroe and Clift – they don't know what the hell they're doing… We don't belong in the same room together.

**CLARK GABLE ON MARILYN MONROE,
MONTGOMERY CLIFT AND ARTHUR MILLER**
(*author of* The Misfits)

We had a great time together on *Habeas Corpus*. Rachel's work was immaculate, scrupulous, detailed; within that rigid framework she had great comic freedom. She took endless pains – I remember her saying two or three times, "Am I taking up too much rehearsal time?" Once she'd got it, she repeated it perfectly, every performance. Her "precision", that's the quality I'd put my finger on.

JEAN MARSH ON RACHEL ROBERTS

Trevor Howard is a new one on everyone. He has been invalided out of the army and…the really terrible thing about him is that he is eight years younger than I am. Isn't it dreadful? When I first realised it I nearly fainted with shock and horror but now I'm getting acclimatised and treat him like a mother.

CELIA JOHNSON ON TREVOR HOWARD
(filming Brief Encounter*)*

Celia [Johnson] and I had totally different methods of work. She always knew precisely what she was doing. That is not to say she didn't vary her performance – she certainly did – but she was like a little clock; she always knew exactly where and how whereas I was rather like a man splashing on the paint and hoping for the best.

MICHAEL HORDERN

I can't work with Welles. If the picture's a hit he will get the credit, and if it's a flop, I'll be blamed.

CAROLE LOMBARD ON ORSON WELLES

When we did a scene together we forgot about technique, camera angles, and microphones. We weren't acting. We were just two people in perfect harmony. Many times I've played with an actress who seemed to be separated from me by a plate-glass window; there was no contact at all. But Myrna, unlike some actresses who think only of themselves, has the happy faculty of being able to listen while the other fellow says his lines. She has the give and take of acting that brings out the best.

WILLIAM POWELL ON MYRNA LOY

I have never in my life worked with a woman who had the smell of drama as this woman has. She is so feminine. She's a man's woman.

JOHN WAYNE ON KATHARINE HEPBURN

He's a very, very good actor in the highbrow sense of the word.

KATHARINE HEPBURN ON JOHN WAYNE

The only way I'd work with Marlon Brando is if he were in rear projection.

JOANNE WOODWARD

I know he's good. I like to see him on the screen. I just don't like working with him.

HUMPHREY BOGART ON ROD STEIGER

I seem to have been unloading all my frustrations over the location [for *Major Dundee*] on poor Dick Harris. In retrospect, I was unfair. It was a gruelling location, and Dick wasn't used to working with either horses or guns. If he was a fuck-up, I was a hard-nosed son of a bitch.

CHARLTON HESTON ON RICHARD HARRIS

She's a monster. If you think she's not strong, you'd better pay attention.

ROBERT MITCHUM ON SARAH MILES

I found her the most obnoxious woman I've ever worked with. She's a very experienced, accomplished actress, a rich woman too. I was no competition to her, she wasn't being upstaged by me. She just decided to make life miserable.

ANTHONY HOPKINS ON SHIRLEY MacLAINE

You can never underestimate him. Not for a minute. He's dangerous to work with, that man, because you never know what he's going to do.

GLENDA JACKSON ON WALTER MATTHAU

Working with Glenda [Jackson] is like being run over by a Bedford truck.

OLIVER REED

Jack Nicholson is the funniest man and the most generous actor I've ever worked with. And the witches – Cher and Michelle [Pfeiffer] and I – got along just brilliantly. Make that super-naturally. Nicholson had fun with *all* the girls.

SUSAN SARANDON
(*filming* The Witches of Eastwick)

I amended the actor's cliché to "Never work with children, animals or Denholm Elliott."

GABRIEL BYRNE

To work with Maggie [Smith] and then with Vanessa [Redgrave] is to go from alpha to omega. They are the Gielgud and the Olivier of our age in the sense that they represent absolute opposites. Vanessa inhabits poetic states and becomes infused with them; but what they are, and where they come from, is entirely mysterious. Maggie, on the other hand, is interested in a particular truth at every moment and she goes at it like a forensic scientist. She never stops.

SIMON CALLOW

Watch her. She'll have that scene from under your feet.

MICHAEL CAINE ON MAGGIE SMITH

I'd heard things people said about Dustin, but I didn't anticipate problems. I mean he's an actor's actor. He's so bright, so brilliant.

TOM CRUISE ON DUSTIN HOFFMAN

[Dustin] can be a pain, very wearying. All he does, morning, noon and night, is work.

HOWARD DUFF ON DUSTIN HOFFMAN

Anyone who has come close to Warren has shed quite a few feathers. He tends to maul you.

LESLIE CARON ON WARREN BEATTY

Mia is a very, very fine actress and does characters very well. Diane doesn't do characters. She does that one thing – her own personality. This is a very strong personality, stronger than Mia's personality. In *Broadway Danny Rose*, Diane could never have played that role, whereas Mia went in and played it beautifully. Diane is a very funny person naturally. Mia is witty, but not as funny as Diane. Diane is so strong comedically that she doesn't need jokes. In fact, she can't even tell jokes. Mia is great at telling jokes, and if I wrote a joke for her she delivered it very beautifully. Diane can't even deliver a joke – she ruins them.

WOODY ALLEN ON MIA FARROW AND DIANE KEATON

ACKNOWLEDGEMENTS

Permission from actors to quote their words, and from authors and publishers to quote from the following works, is gratefully acknowledged:

Noël Coward on Gertrude Lawrence copyright © 1967 the estate of Noël Coward, courtesy Michael Imison Playwrights Ltd; Virginia McKenna for her quote from *Peter Finch: A Biography* by Trader Faulkner; Ernest Borgnine on Spencer Tracy, from 'Lee Marvin's Great, Goddamned Moments of the Big Kavoom' by Grover Lewis (*Rolling Stone*, 21.12. 1972), courtesy Straight Arrow Publishers Inc 1972, all rights reserved; *Stage People* by Roger Lewis, Weidenfeld & Nicolson 1982; Alan Bates; Suzanne Bertish; Ian Richardson; Eileen Atkins; *The Independent* for permission to quote from Sheila Johnston's interview with Chazz Palminteri; *Bob Hoskins – An Unlikely Hero* by Karen Moline (Sidgwick & Jackson 1988), courtesy The Jane Gregory Agency; *An Actor and His Time* by John Gielgud (Sidgwick & Jackson); Peter Wyngarde; *I Must Be In There Somewhere* by Joss Ackland (Hodder & Stoughton, London 1989), courtesy Dinah Weiner; *Brando: Songs My Mother Taught Me* by Marlon Brando, copyright © Marlon Brando 1994, Random House Inc; *A World Elsewhere* by Michael Hordern, copyright © 1993 Michael Hordern and Patricia England, courtesy Michael O'Mara Books Ltd; Lady Olivier; *Confessions of an Actor* by Laurence Olivier, Weidenfeld & Nicolson 1982; *The Actor's Life* by Charlton Heston, copyright © 1978 Charlton Heston, courtesy International Creative Management Inc; Derek Jacobi on Edith Evans/Noël Coward on Derek Jacobi, courtesy *The Independent*; *Topol on Topol*, Weidenfeld & Nicolson 1981; Donald Sinden; Ian McKellen; *The Noël Coward Diaries* (ed Graham Payn & Sheridan Morley), Weidenfeld & Nicolson 1982; *Snakes and Ladders* by Dirk Bogarde (Chatto & Windus 1978), Random House; *Writing Home* by Alan Bennett, Faber & Faber Ltd 1994, reprinted by permission of Peters, Fraser and Dunlop Group Ltd; *It's Only A Movie, Ingrid* by Alexander Walker, courtesy of the author; *The Player* by Lillian Ross copyright © 1961 Lillian Ross, copyright © 1962 Lillian Ross and Helen Ross, originally published by Simon & Schuster, used by permission of Lillian Ross; *Dear Me* by Peter Ustinov (Heinemann 1977), courtesy Pavor S.A; *Memoirs of a Professional Cad* by George Sanders, Putnams 1960, copyright © The Putnam Publishing Group; Rita Tushingham; *Marlene Dietrich: My Life*, Weidenfeld & Nicolson 1989; *Life is Too Short* by Mickey Rooney, Random House Inc/Random House UK Ltd; Jean Marsh; *Celia Johnson* by Kate Fleming, Weidenfeld & Nicolson 1991; *Anthony Hopkins: A Biography* by Quentin Falk (Virgin), courtesy of the author; Simon Callow; *The Independent on Sunday* for permission to quote from Simon Garfield's article on Woody Allen.